DO ONE THING EVERY DAY TO SIMPLIFY YOUR LIFE

A Journal for Living Better

This journal belongs to:

_____

SIMPLICITY IS LIGHT, CAREFREE, NEAT, AND LOVING—NOT A SELF-PUNISHING ASCETIC TRIP.

Gary Snyder

Simplicity is a balance, tricky but attainable. In *Do One Thing Every Day to Simplify Your Life*, inspiring quotes, practical advice, and challenging prompts will steer you toward this happy way of being and away from the pitfalls of strict self-denial.

Simplicity is "light," Snyder writes. Look to the words about nature and language inside this book and to the features that urge you to explore your senses, such as Simple Sounds and Simple Sights. The entries under Simple Tips and K.I.S.S (Keep It Simple, Stupid) will make everyday life more "carefree." They offer systems to clear your physical space, from your inbox to your backpack, and specific efficiencies for unmatched socks, chaotic linens, and lost bills. The entries under Simple Mind-set will help to clear your mind.

For advice on being "neat," read the words of nineteenth century designer William Morris and today's tidying guru Marie Kondo. Also consult the feature Back to Basics to reduce your oversupply of tools, clothing, and other possessions by identifying the essentials. Finally, simplicity, according to Snyder, means "loving" yourself, others, and the world around you. Look for quotes and prompts throughout this book that elicit self-understanding and gratitude and the feature Simple Gifts, with suggestions of small treasures to give to someone dear.

Guiding you on this journey to simplify your physical and mental life are writers, philosophers, chefs, politicians, musicians, scientists, artists, and celebrities, from ancient times to the present, who have dropped the excess baggage from their own lives while gathering extra joy.

Where should you start? The unnumbered pages of this book are meant to be flipped through and sampled according to your mood with two exceptions. Begin by marking your place on the meter below. Then rate yourself again, on the meter at the end of the book, after a year of *doing one thing every day to simplify your life.*

DATE: ___ / ___ / ___

RATE YOUR LIFE TODAY FROM "OVERLY COMPLICATED" TO "PERFECTLY SIMPLE."

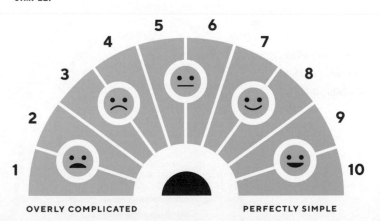

Simplify, simplify, simplify! I say, let your affairs be as two or three, and not a hundred or a thousand; instead of a million count half a dozen, and keep your accounts on your thumb-nail.

Henry David Thoreau

Write your affairs
for today on this
thumbnail:

"Do nothing but what is necessary;"
[says Democritus]. . . . For by this rule a man has the
double pleasure of making his actions good and few into
the bargain. . . . And therefore before a man sets forward,
he should ask himself this question, "Am I not upon
the verge of something unnecessary?"

Marcus Aurelius Antoninus

Something unnecessary I eliminated today:

DATE: ___ / ___ / ___

KEEP IT SIMPLE, (STUPID).

K.I.S.S.
Household

A single bottle of distilled white vinegar can be used for multiple chores around the house. It is also environmentally safe and inexpensive.

Today, with a single bottle of vinegar, I:

- [ ] disinfected the refrigerator, microwave, and stove (1 part vinegar to 3 parts hot water)

- [ ] washed my windows (equal parts vinegar and water)

- [ ] killed weeds (applied full strength)

- [ ] cleaned sponges (soaked full strength)

- [ ] got rid of deodorant and wine stains (applied full strength and laundered after)

- [ ] rinsed my hair (1 to 2 tablespoons vinegar to 1 cup water)

- [ ] unclogged a sink (applied full strength)

- [ ] got rid of kitchen odor (simmer ½ cup vinegar for 30 to 45 minutes)

DATE: __/__/__

LESS IS MORE.

Ludwig Mies van der Rohe

Today I replaced these commercial household cleaners with a single bottle of distilled white vinegar:

_____

_____

_____

_____

_____

THE ART OF BEING WISE IS THE ART OF KNOWING WHAT TO OVERLOOK.

William James

I OVERLOOKED THIS DEMAND AT WORK TODAY:

_____

_____

_____

_____

_____

_____

I OVERLOOKED THIS SOCIAL DEMAND TODAY:

_____

_____

_____

_____

_____

_____

I believe the road to hell is paved with adverbs, and I will shout it from the rooftops.

Stephen King

Choose better verbs below, so that you can eliminate the unnecessary adverbs (e.g., ran quickly ⟶ dashed):

ate energetically ⟶ _____

slept lightly ⟶ _____

disliked intensely ⟶ _____

cleaned vigorously ⟶ _____

Writing is easy.
All you have to do is cross out the wrong words.

Mark Twain

Cross out the seven wrong words from the first line of the Gettysburg Address:

Four score and seven long years ago our fathers brought back and forth, upon this verdant continent, a spanking new nation, conceived in Liberty, and dedicated to the serious proposition that all men are created approximately equal.

Simple Gifts

Address the tag for a simple gift you gave today:

VEGETABLE SEEDS

to:

service

to:

other

to:

SEASHELL

to:

SONG

to:

FRIENDSHIP BRACELET

to:

MASSAGE

to: _____

FAVORITE BOOK

to:

One can get just as much exultation in losing oneself in a little thing as in a big thing. It is nice to think how one can be recklessly lost in a daisy!

Anne Morrow Lindbergh

Today I was recklessly lost in this little thing:

_____

_____

_____

_____

_____

He was one of the greatest scientists the world has ever known, yet if I had to convey the essence of Albert Einstein in a single word, I would choose *simplicity*.

Banesh Hoffmann

The person whose essence I could describe as "simplicity":

_____

_____

_____

_____

_____

Most of the fundamental ideas of science are essentially simple, and may, as a rule, be expressed in a language comprehensible to everyone.

Albert Einstein

Express something sophisticated in a language comprehensible to everyone:

_____

_____

_____

_____

_____

"What do you like doing best in the world, Pooh?" [asked Christopher Robin.]

"What I like best in the whole world is Me and Piglet going to see You, and You saying 'What about a little something?' and Me saying, 'Well, I shouldn't mind a little something, should you, Piglet,' and it being a hummy sort of day outside, and birds singing."

A. A. Milne

DATE: __ / __ / __

A SIMPLE ENCOUNTER WITH A FRIEND THAT MADE THIS DAY "HUMMY":

_____

_____

_____

_____

_____

_____

DATE: __ / __ / __

A LITTLE SOMETHING I SHARED WITH A FRIEND TODAY:

_____

_____

_____

_____

_____

_____

THE MOON BELONGS TO EVERYONE, THE BEST THINGS IN LIFE ARE FREE.

Buddy DeSylva and Lew Brown

A priceless gift I received today:

_____

_____

_____

_____

_____

The truly rich are those who enjoy what they have.

Yiddish proverb

I am truly rich because I enjoyed this today:

_____

_____

_____

_____

_____

Simple tips:
One In, One Out

When you get something new, get rid of something old.

Today I got a new _____

and threw out this old _____. Yay!

OUT WITH THE OLD, IN WITH THE NEW.

English idiom

Today I tossed out this old _____

and got this new _____ .

A SMILE IS THE BEST MAKEUP ANY GIRL CAN WEAR.

Marilyn Monroe

Draw a picture of
yourself with your
"best makeup":

To me more dear,
      congenial to my heart,
One native charm,
      than all the gloss of art.

Oliver Goldsmith

A simple trait that charms my heart: ☐ sense of humor

☐ kindness

☐ generosity

☐ _____

other

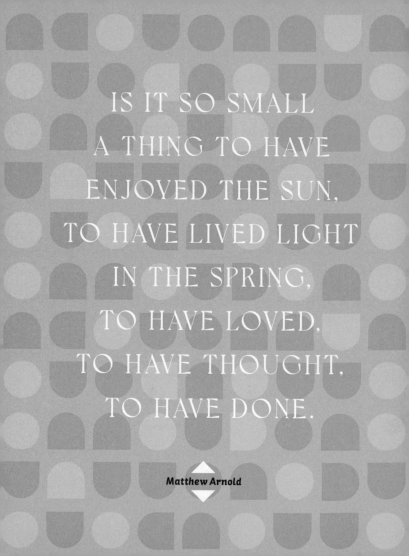

IS IT SO SMALL
A THING TO HAVE
ENJOYED THE SUN,
TO HAVE LIVED LIGHT
IN THE SPRING,
TO HAVE LOVED,
TO HAVE THOUGHT,
TO HAVE DONE.

Matthew Arnold

DATE: ___ / ___ / ___

A BIT OF NATURE I ENJOYED TODAY:

_____

_____

_____

DATE: ___ / ___ / ___

SOMEONE I LOVED TODAY:

_____

_____

_____

DATE: ___ / ___ / ___

ONE THING I ACCOMPLISHED TODAY:

_____

_____

_____

IT DOES NOT NEED THAT A POEM SHOULD BE LONG. EVERY WORD WAS ONCE A POEM.

Ralph Waldo Emerson

A word that is like a poem for me: _____

I LIKE AN EMPTY WALL BECAUSE I CAN IMAGINE WHAT I LIKE ON IT.

Georgia O'Keeffe

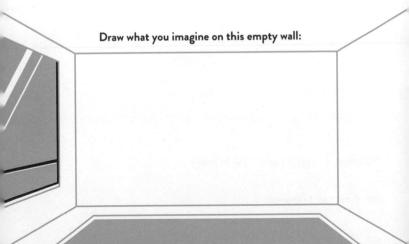

Draw what you imagine on this empty wall:

DATE: __ / __ / __

SIMPLE MIND-SET

SAY "NO"

To devote yourself to a single passion or project requires an emphatic "yes" to that, and an equally emphatic "no" to even well-meaning interferences.

A passion or project I said "Yes" to today: _____

Interferences I rejected: _____

_____

The art of leadership is saying no, not yes. It is very easy to say Yes.

Tony Blair

My goal at work today: _____

What I said "no" to today: _____

What I accomplished: _____

It takes a lot of time to be a genius, you have to sit around so much doing nothing, really doing nothing.

Gertrude Stein

Today I sat around doing nothing and discovered this:

_____

_____

_____

_____

_____

Things which matter most must never be at the mercy of things which matter least.

Johann Wolfgang von Goethe

What mattered most today:

_____

_____

_____

_____

_____

DATE: ___ /___ /___

BELONGINGS THAT MAKE ME HAPPY:

_____

_____

_____

_____

_____

_____

DATE: ___ /___ /___

BELONGINGS I SHOULD THROW AWAY:

_____

_____

_____

_____

_____

_____

I was obsessed with what I could throw away. One day, . . . I heard a mysterious voice, like some god of tidying, telling me to look at my things more closely. And I realized my mistake: I was only looking for things to throw out. What I should be doing is finding the things I want to keep. Identifying the things that make you happy: that is the work of tidying.

Marie Kondo

I love a life whose plot is simple,
And does not thicken with every pimple.

Henry David Thoreau

To live more simply, I ignored these "pimples" on the plot of my life today:

_____

_____

_____

_____

_____

Life has a very simple plot. First you're here, and then you're not.

Eric Idle

My life had this very simple plot today:

_____

_____

_____

_____

_____

K.I.S.S.
Anxiety

To release anxiety, use the simple 4-7-8 breathing technique, also known as relaxing breath: Breathe in for 4 seconds; hold the breath for 7 seconds; exhale for 8 seconds.

☐ Did it. Ahhhhh.

Breathing in,
I calm my body.
Breathing out, I smile.

Thich Nhat Hanh

How I calmed my body today: _____

_____

_____

_____

_____

_____

*Blessed is the man who,
having nothing to say,
abstains from giving us
wordy evidence of the fact.*

George Eliot

A friend whose laconic style I admire:

_____

_____

For brevity is very good,
When we are, or are
not understood.

Samuel Butler

A public figure whose laconic style I admire:

_____

_____

THE IMPORTANT
THINGS ARE ALWAYS
SIMPLE; THE SIMPLE ARE
ALWAYS HARD.

Murphy's Laws of Combat

DATE: ___ / ___ / ___

AN IMPORTANT THING THAT TURNED OUT TO BE SIMPLE TODAY:

_____

_____

_____

_____

_____

_____

DATE: ___ / ___ / ___

A SIMPLE THING THAT TURNED OUT TO BE HARD TODAY:

_____

_____

_____

_____

_____

_____

If I had but two loaves of bread
I would sell one of them and buy
White Hyacinths to feed my soul.

Elbert Hubbard

Flowers that fed my soul today:

_____

_____

_____

_____

_____

CHOOSE SUCH PLEASURES AS RECREATE MUCH AND COST LITTLE.

Thomas Fuller, attributed

A simple, free recreation that brought me pleasure today:

_____

_____

_____

_____

_____

BACK TO BASICS
KITCHENWARE:

Reduce your kitchen clutter. All you need to prepare simple, healthy, delicious meals are these 10 basic tools. Mark the ones you already own.

- ☐ stainless-steel 10-inch skillet
- ☐ heavy 8-quart pot
- ☐ sheet tray
- ☐ cutting board
- ☐ chef's knife
- ☐ peeler
- ☐ fine-mesh sieve
- ☐ large spoon
- ☐ dry and liquid measuring cups
- ☐ measuring spoons

I never see any home cooking. All I get is fancy stuff.

Prince Philip, Duke of Edinburgh

A tasty, nutritious, un-fancy dish I made today with basic kitchen tools:

_____

_____

_____

FIRST THOUGHT, BEST THOUGHT.

Allen Ginsberg, attributed

Quick write!

_____

_____

_____

_____

_____

Just dash something down if you see a blank canvas staring at you with a certain imbecility.

Vincent van Gogh

Quick draw!

DATE: ___ / ___ / ___

I CAN DO WITHOUT THESE GOODS:

_____

_____

_____

_____

_____

_____

DATE: ___ / ___ / ___

I CAN DO WITHOUT THESE SERVICES:

_____

_____

_____

_____

_____

_____

HOW MANY THINGS CAN I DO WITHOUT?

Socrates

I prefer to explore the most intimate moments, the smaller, crystallized details we all hinge our lives on.

Rita Dove

What I discovered from exploring a small detail of my life today:

_____

_____

_____

_____

_____

Often ornateness
    goes with greatness;
Oftener felicity
    comes of simplicity.

William Watson

I admire this ornate building:

_____

I admire this simple building even more:

_____

Simple tips:
Water Bottle

If you carry a water bottle everywhere, you can refill it at your convenience and save money.

You will also save the world from mounting plastic litter.

☐ Today I commit to carrying a water bottle.

We never know the worth of water till the well is dry.

Thomas Fuller

I know the worth of water to keep my body functioning properly.

I try to drink _____ glasses a day.

The only things we ever keep
Are what we give away.

Louis Ginsberg

What I gave away today that I will cherish in my memory:

_____

_____

_____

_____

_____

DATE: __ / __ / __

WHO SHUTS HIS HAND, HATH LOST HIS GOLD; WHO OPENS IT, HATH IT TWICE TOLD.

George Herbert

An openhanded gesture I made today:

_____

_____

_____

_____

_____

HAVE NOTHING
IN YOUR HOUSE
THAT YOU DO
NOT KNOW TO
BE USEFUL, OR
BELIEVE TO BE
BEAUTIFUL.

William Morris

DATE: ___/___/___

SOMETHING I WILL KEEP IN MY HOUSE BECAUSE IT IS USEFUL OR BEAUTIFUL:

_____

_____

_____

_____

_____

DATE: ___/___/___

SOMETHING I WILL GIVE AWAY BECAUSE TO ME IT IS USELESS OR UGLY:

_____

_____

_____

_____

_____

_____

"Silence," it has been said by one writer, "is a virtue which renders us agreeable to our fellow-creatures."

Samuel Butler

I was agreeably silent among my "fellow-creatures" today because:

_____

_____

_____

_____

_____

Noise proves nothing. Often a hen who has merely laid an egg cackles as if she laid an asteroid.

Mark Twain

Someone who was loud but ineffective today:

_____

_____

_____

_____

_____

DATE: __/__/__

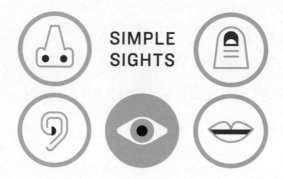

SIMPLE SIGHTS

| **Bob Thiele and George David Weiss** | I see skies of blue and clouds of white . . . and I think to myself what a wonderful world. |

What I see every day that makes me think, "What a wonderful world":

_____

_____

_____

MY HEART LEAPS UP
WHEN I BEHOLD
A RAINBOW IN THE SKY.

William Wordsworth

A natural wonder that made my heart leap up today:

_____

_____

_____

DATE: ___ / ___ / ___

Above all, do not lose your desire to walk. Every day
I walk myself into a state of well-being and walk away
from every illness. I have walked myself into my best
thoughts, and I know of no thought so burdensome
that one cannot walk away from it.

Søren Kierkegaard

How my walk increased my well-being today:

_____

_____

_____

_____

_____

I HAVE TWO DOCTORS, MY LEFT LEG AND MY RIGHT.

George M. Trevelyan

How my walk improved my health today:

_____

_____

_____

_____

_____

DATE: ___ / ___ / ___

A REVIEW OF MY FAVORITE BOOK IN FOUR WORDS:

_____

_____

_____

_____

DATE: ___ / ___ / ___

A REVIEW OF MY FAVORITE ☐ SONG ☐ PODCAST ☐ PAINTING ☐ PERFORMANCE IN FOUR WORDS:

_____

_____

_____

_____

THE WORDS "KISS KISS
BANG BANG," WHICH
I SAW ON AN ITALIAN MOVIE
POSTER, ARE PERHAPS
THE BRIEFEST STATEMENT
IMAGINABLE OF THE BASIC
APPEAL OF MOVIES.

Pauline Kael

I never loved a dear Gazelle—
Nor anything that cost me much:
High prices profit those who sell,
But why should I be fond of such.

Lewis Carroll

Luxuries that never tempted me:

_____

_____

_____

_____

_____

DATE: __ /__ /__

THE SADDEST THING I CAN IMAGINE IS TO GET USED TO LUXURY.

Charlie Chaplin

A modest pleasure that makes me happy:

_____

_____

_____

_____

_____

K.I.S.S.
Socks

KEEP IT SIMPLE, (STUPID).

If you buy socks in only one color, you will always be able to match.

From now on, I will buy socks in only this color:

_____

If thou art clean and warm, it is sufficient.

William Penn

I have _____ mismatched socks, but they are clean
and warm, and that is sufficient.

Simplicity is light, carefree, neat, and loving—not a self-punishing ascetic trip.

Gary Snyder

A simple pleasure that denied me nothing:

_____

_____

_____

_____

_____

DATE: __ / __ / __

A little of what you fancy does you good.

Fred W. Leigh

What I fancied today:

_____

_____

_____

_____

_____

A SINGLE
ROSE CAN BE
MY GARDEN . . .
A SINGLE FRIEND,
MY WORLD.

Leo Buscaglia

A SINGLE FLOWER THAT
IS MY GARDEN:

_____

A SINGLE FRIEND
WHO IS MY WORLD:

_____

Simplicity is the keynote of all true elegance.

Coco Chanel

My most elegant piece of clothing:

_____

_____

_____

_____

_____

ELEGANCE IS REFUSAL.

Diana Vreeland, attributed

What I eliminated from my outfit today:

_____

_____

_____

_____

_____

Simple Gifts

Address the tag
for a simple gift
you gave today:

BOOKMARK

to:

FLOWER SEEDS

to:

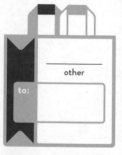

_____ other

to:

CHOCOLATE ON THE BED PILLOW

to:

BEAUTIFUL SCENT

to:

POEM

to:

BIRD'S FEATHER

to: _____

DAISY CHAIN

to:

A GIFT, THOUGH SMALL, IS WELCOME.

Homer

This small gift was especially welcome today:

_____

_____

_____

_____

_____

I was raised to feel that doing nothing was a sin. I had to learn to do nothing.

Jenny Joseph

Why doing nothing was a blessing today:

_____

_____

_____

_____

_____

Idleness . . . is so far from being the root of evil that it is rather the true good.

Søren Kierkegaard

How my idleness led to true good today:

_____

_____

_____

_____

_____

DATE: ___ / ___ / ___

HOW I ELIMINATED BUSYWORK FROM MY PERSONAL LIFE TODAY:

_____

_____

_____

_____

_____

_____

DATE: ___ / ___ / ___

HOW I ELIMINATED BUSYWORK FROM MY WORK LIFE TODAY:

_____

_____

_____

_____

_____

_____

EXTREME BUSYNESS,
WHETHER AT SCHOOL
OR COLLEGE, KIRK
[CHURCH] OR MARKET,
IS A SYMPTOM OF
DEFICIENT VITALITY.

Robert Louis Stevenson

DATE: __ / __ / __

The best number for a dinner party is two—myself and a dam' good head waiter.

Nubar Gulbenkian

The best number for *my* dinner party:

_____

_____

_____

_____

_____

DATE: ___ / ___ / ___

But anythin' for a quiet life, as the man said ven he took the sitivation at the lighthouse.

Charles Dickens

Where I go to be alone:

_____

_____

_____

_____

_____

Simple tips:
Financial Planning

Simplify your financial planning by using the 50/30/20 rule: spend 50 percent of your monthly income on living expenses and 30 percent on your lifestyle, and save 20 percent.

Month of _____

50 percent of my monthly income is $ _____.

My living expenses were $ _____.

30 percent of my monthly income is $ _____.

My lifestyle expenses were $ _____.

20 percent of my monthly income is $ _____.

My savings were $ _____.

It's not your salary that makes you rich, it's your spending habits.

Charles Jaffe

My spending habits make me feel ☐ rich ☐ poor because:

_____

_____

_____

_____

_____

It has long been an axiom of mine that the little things are infinitely the most important.

Sir Arthur Conan Doyle

An important little thing I discovered today:

_____

_____

_____

_____

_____

There are no little things.
"Little things," so called,
are the hinges of the universe.

Fanny Fern

A little thing that turned into something big today:

_____

_____

_____

_____

_____

I DO NOT
AGREE WITH
THE BIG WAY
OF DOING
THINGS.

Mother Teresa

DATE: ___/___/___

A SMALL KIND ACT I DID TODAY:

_____

_____

_____

_____

_____

DATE: ___/___/___

A SMALL KINDNESS THAT TOUCHED ME GREATLY TODAY:

_____

_____

_____

_____

_____

_____

For we brought nothing into this world, and it is certain we can carry nothing out.

The Bible

My wishes for the worldly belongings I will leave:

_____

_____

_____

_____

_____

DATE: ___/___/___

There is nothing quite so good as burial at sea. It is simple, tidy, and not very incriminating.

Alfred Hitchcock

Describe something simple, tidy, and not very incriminating:

_____

_____

_____

_____

_____

SIMPLE MIND-SET

SLOW DOWN

Slowing down the pace of your life for even half an hour a day allows room for your body to refuel and for your mind to reflect on both your inner and outer life and to expand into unexplored corners. You can do this simply by silencing the music as you walk or drive, or turning off your phone as you wait in line at a store.

How I slowed down today:

_____

_____

What I discovered:

_____

_____

WHAT IS THIS LIFE IF, FULL OF CARE, WE HAVE NO TIME TO STAND AND STARE.

W. H. Davies

How long I sat and stared today:

_____

_____

What I discovered:

_____

_____

All organization is and must be grounded on the idea of exclusion and prohibition just as two objects cannot occupy the same space.

Arthur Miller

What I excluded to simplify my work life today:

_____

_____

_____

_____

_____

TO ATTAIN KNOWLEDGE, ADD THINGS EVERY DAY. TO ATTAIN WISDOM, SUBTRACT THINGS EVERY DAY.

Lao-tzu

What I learned when I subtracted something today:

_____

_____

_____

_____

_____

A SIMPLE TASTE THAT DID NOT COME NATURALLY:

A WAY I COMPLICATE MY LIFE UNNECESSARILY:

SIMPLICITY
IS AN ACQUIRED
TASTE. MANKIND,
LEFT FREE,
INSTINCTIVELY
COMPLICATES
LIFE.

Katherine F. Gerould

A sheltered life can be a daring life as well. For all serious daring starts from within.

Eudora Welty

How I showed daring in my sheltered life today:

_____

_____

_____

_____

_____

Almost any man may, like the spider, spin from his own inwards his own airy citadel.

John Keats

Something I spun out today:

_____

_____

_____

_____

_____

KEEP IT SIMPLE, (STUPID).

K.I.S.S.
Words

Use simple words to express yourself rather than long ones. Replace the long words below with three-letter words.

surreptitious   __ __ __

disconsolate   __ __ __

incensed   __ __ __

expire   __ __ __

venture   __ __ __

articulate   __ __ __

cartograph   __ __ __

scintilla   __ __ __

pinnacle   __ __ __

prevaricate   __ __ __

delectation   __ __ __

Answers : sly, sad, mad, die, bet, say, map, bit, top, lie, joy

Never use a long word where a short one will do.

George Orwell

Translate this back into a simple line of well-known poetry:

I conjecture that I shall under no circumstances discern a literary verse form as ravishing as an arboreal growth.

Answer: I think that I shall never see a poem lovely as a tree.

WASTE IS A SPIRITUAL THING AND HARMS THE SOUL AS WELL AS THE POCKETBOOK.

Kathleen Norris

No longer being wasteful with _____ lifted my spirit, and
it saved me $ _____

Unnecessary possessions are unnecessary burdens. If you have them, you have to take care of them!

Peace Pilgrim

An unnecessary possession I got rid of today: _____

IF YOU CAN'T REDUCE
A DIFFICULT ENGINEERING
PROBLEM TO JUST ONE
8 1/2 × 11-INCH SHEET
OF PAPER, YOU WILL
NEVER UNDERSTAND IT.

Ralph Brazelton Peck

DATE: ___ / ___ / ___

I REDUCED THIS TECH PROBLEM TO THE BOX BELOW:

DATE: ___ / ___ / ___

I REDUCED THIS _____ PROBLEM TO THE BOX BELOW:

DATE: __/__/__

THANKFUL FOR SMALL MERCIES.

James Joyce

I was thankful for this small mercy today:

_____

_____

_____

_____

_____

Human felicity is produced not so much by the great pieces of good fortune that seldom happen, as by little advantages that occur every day.

Benjamin Franklin

A little daily advantage that made me happy today:

_____

_____

_____

_____

_____

BACK TO BASICS
WORK-LIFE ESSENTIALS:

Clean out your closet. Meghan Markle, Duchess of Sussex, created this capsule wardrobe for a charity that serves women returning to work. Mark how many of each item you have in your work wardrobe and how many you actually use. (You may choose to replace the dress with a suit.)

 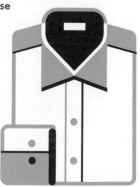

☐ **Tailored white shirt:** I have _____ ; I use _____ .

☐ **Blazer:** I have _____ ; I use _____ .

☐ **Classic black trousers:** I have: _____ ; I use _____ .

☐ **Crepe shift dress:** I have _____ ; I use _____ .

☐ **Leather tote:** I have _____ ; I use _____ .

YOU CAN HAVE TOO MUCH OF A GOOD THING.

Proverb

What I did with the excess from my wardrobe:

_____

_____

_____

_____

_____

The world has become too full of many things, an over furnished room.

Freya Stark

Something unnecessary I eliminated from my world:

_____

_____

_____

_____

_____

One can furnish a room very luxuriously by taking out furniture rather than putting it in.

Francis Jourdain

Cross out the excess furniture

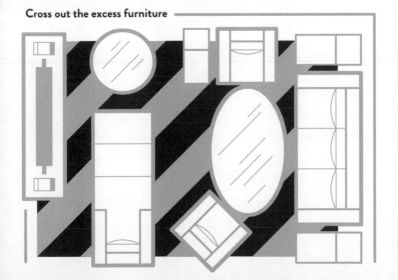

DATE: ___ / ___ / ___

WE LOOK TOO MUCH TO CONCERTS. THIS SOUND FROM NATURE IS ENOUGH:

_____

_____

_____

_____

_____

_____

DATE: ___ / ___ / ___

WE LOOK TOO MUCH TO BALLET. THIS MOVEMENT IN NATURE IS ENOUGH:

_____

_____

_____

_____

_____

_____

WE LOOK
TOO MUCH TO
MUSEUMS. THE
SUN COMING UP IN
THE MORNING IS
ENOUGH.

Ralph Ellison

I like to go to Marshall Field's in Chicago just to see how many things there are in the world that I do not want.

Mother Mary Madeleva

When I go to _____, **I see many things I do not want:**

_____

_____

_____

_____

_____

We are the slaves of objects around us.

Johann Wolfgang von Goethe

These objects require more work than they are worth:

_____

_____

_____

_____

_____

Simple tips:
Communications

Take control of your communications. Set specific times and specific limits for sending and receiving e-mails, texts, phone calls, and any other communications.

Device:	Schedule:	Time Limit:

By failing to prepare, you are preparing to fail.

Benjamin Franklin

Because I simplified my communications, I was able to accomplish this today:

_____

_____

_____

_____

_____

My gift is my song and this one's for you.

Elton John and Bernie Taupin

I gave this of my talent today:

_____

_____

_____

_____

_____

There is only one real deprivation, I decided
this morning, and that is not to be able
to give one's gifts to those one loves most.

May Sarton

Today I was able to give my gift to someone I love most:

_____

_____

_____

_____

_____

A MULTITUDE
OF SMALL
DELIGHTS
CONSTITUTES
HAPPINESS.

Charles Baudelaire

DATE: ___/___/___

SMALL DELIGHT #1:

_____

_____

SMALL DELIGHT #2

_____

_____

SMALL DELIGHT #3:

_____

_____

DATE: ___/___/___

MORE SMALL DELIGHTS:

_____

_____

_____

_____

The best things carried to excess are wrong.

Charles Churchill

Instead of overdoing _____ today,

I _____ .

IN CHARITY THERE IS NO EXCESS.

Francis Bacon

Today I gave to this charity:

_____

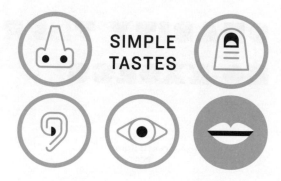

SIMPLE TASTES

| Chinese proverb | Sour, sweet, bitter, pungent, all must be tasted. |

I tasted these simple flavors today:

sour _____

sweet _____

bitter _____

pungent _____

Do the small things of life with a relaxed awareness. When you are eating, eat totally—chew totally, taste totally, smell totally. Touch your bread, feel the texture. Smell the bread, smell the flavor. Chew it, let it dissolve into your being, and remain conscious—and you are meditating.

Osho

How I enjoyed a simple food totally today:

_____

_____

_____

_____

Minds, like bodies, will often fall into a pimpled, ill-conditioned state from mere excess of comfort.

Charles Dickens

A simple way I keep my mind fit:

_____

_____

_____

_____

_____

PERHAPS TOO MUCH OF EVERYTHING IS AS BAD AS TOO LITTLE.

Edna Ferber

Too much of _____ **is as bad as too little:**

_____

_____

_____

_____

_____

DATE: ___ /___ /___

A SMALL MEMORY OF NATURE I WILL TAKE WITH ME WHEN I DIE:

DATE: ___ /___ /___

A SMALL MEMORY OF MY CHILDHOOD I WILL TAKE WITH ME WHEN I DIE:

THE SHAPE OF A PARTICULAR
HILL, A ROAD IN THE TOWN IN
WHICH WE LIVED AS CHILDREN,
THE MOVEMENT OF WIND IN
GRASS. THE THINGS WE SHALL
TAKE WITH US WHEN WE
DIE WILL NEARLY ALL BE
SMALL THINGS.

Storm Jameson

Sweet is the breath of vernal shower,

The bee's collected treasures sweet,

Sweet music's melting fall, but sweeter yet

The still small voice of gratitude.

Thomas Gray

A small voice of gratitude I heard today:

Giving presents is a talent:
to know what a person wants,
to know when and how to get it,
to give it lovingly and well.

Pamela Glenconner

How I used my talent for gift-giving today:

_____

_____

_____

_____

_____

DATE: __/__/__

KEEP IT SIMPLE, (STUPID).

K.I.S.S.
Dinner

This simple recipe requires only two ingredients.

Chicken Mexicano: Place boneless chicken breasts in a baking dish and smother with a jar of salsa. Bake at 375°F for 40 minutes.

Today I made this simple dish with a complex flavor:

_____

_____

_____

DATE: __/__/__

Good food is very often, even most often, simple food.

Anthony Bourdain

My favorite recipe for simple food: _____

_____

_____

_____

[The "classic formula" for a novel:] A beginning, a muddle, and an end.

Philip Larkin

My favorite novel,_____:

beginning:_____

muddle:_____

_____

end:_____

Think of it [a first sentence] as analogous to a good country breakfast: what we want is something simple, but nourishing to the imagination.

Larry McMurtry

My favorite first sentence:

_____

_____

_____

_____

_____

MY
PHILOSOPHY?
SIMPLICITY PLUS
VARIETY.

Hank Stram

DATE: ___ / ___ / ___

TODAY I FOUND THIS SIMPLE WAY TO:

_____

_____

_____

_____

_____

_____

DATE: ___ / ___ / ___

HOW I ADDED VARIETY TO MY SIMPLE _____ STRATEGY TODAY:

_____

_____

_____

_____

_____

_____

DATE: __/__/__

*The discovery of a new
dish does more for human
happiness than the discovery
of a star.*

Jean Anthelme Brillat-Savarin

A simple new dish I discovered today:

_____

_____

_____

_____

_____

I have often said that I wish I had invented blue jeans: the most spectacular, the most practical, the most relaxed and nonchalant. They have expression, modesty, sex appeal, simplicity—all I hope for in my clothes.

Yves Saint Laurent

A simple piece of clothing I own that is spectacular, practical, relaxed, and nonchalant:

_____

_____

_____

_____

_____

Simple Gifts

Address the tag for a simple gift you gave today:

DRAWING
to:

CUP OF COCOA
to:

other
to:

SINGLE ROSE
to:

HOMEMADE COOKIES
to:

RECITATION
to:

WALK TO SEE A BEAUTIFUL SIGHT
to: _____

HAIR RIBBON
to:

DATE: ___ / ___ / ___

I am beginning to learn that it is
the sweet, simple things of life which
are the real ones after all.

Laura Ingalls Wilder

A sweet, simple gift I appreciated today:

_____

_____

_____

_____

_____

We shall have to learn to refrain from doing things merely because we know how to do them.

Theodore Fox

I know how to _____ ,

but it is simpler just to:

_____

_____

_____

_____

_____

The simpler I keep things, the better I play.

Nancy Lopez

A simple move I use in _____

(sport)

that improves my play:

_____

_____

_____

_____

_____

DATE: __/__/__

WHAT I SAVED TODAY:

_____

_____

_____

_____

_____

_____

DATE: __/__/__

WHAT I SPENT MY SAVINGS ON TODAY:

_____

_____

_____

_____

_____

_____

SPARE WELL AND HAVE TO SPEND.

Proverb

Of every four words I write, I strike out three.

Nicolas Boileau

Make Boileau's statement even simpler by striking out three words:

_____

_____

_____

_____

The waste basket is a writer's best friend.

Isaac Bashevis Singer

Why the computer "trash" was my best friend today:

_____

_____

_____

_____

_____

Simple tips:
Bedsheets

Straight from the dryer, put the folded top and bottom sheets and one pillowcase inside the other pillowcase so you don't have to search later for a matching set.

◯ Did it.

In a small space, you want to keep
the bedding as simple as possible
so it looks clean, calm, and collected.

Nate Berkus

Draw bedding for a bed in the smallest room of your house:

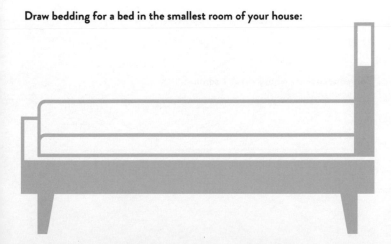

VIRTUE IS LIKE A RICH STONE, BEST PLAIN SET.

Francis Bacon

Someone modest whose virtue I admire:

_____

_____

_____

_____

_____

DATE: ___/___/___

DO GOOD BY STEALTH, AND BLUSH TO FIND IT FAME.

Alexander Pope

I discovered today that _____ did this good deed anonymously:

_____

_____

_____

_____

_____

HAVE SOMETHING
TO SAY, AND SAY
IT AS CLEARLY AS
YOU CAN. THAT IS
THE ONLY SECRET
OF STYLE.

Matthew Arnold

DATE: ___ / ___ / ___

WHAT WAS CASEY STENGEL, FAMOUS MANAGER OF THE YANKEES, TRYING TO SAY HERE? "MOST PEOPLE MY AGE ARE DEAD AT THE PRESENT TIME."

DATE: ___ / ___ / ___

REWRITE STENGEL'S STATEMENT (ABOVE) AS CLEARLY AS YOU CAN:

What should I do with your strong, manly, spirited
sketches, full of variety & glow?—How could
I possibly join them on to the little bit (two inches
wide) of ivory on which I work with so fine a brush,
as produces little effect after much labour?

Jane Austen

In this 2-inch box,
make a sketch of
someone you know.

The Atlantic's too big for me.
A creek's got more of the sea in it,
for people who want to turn it
into poetry.

Edith Wharton

Something small that inspires me more than something grand:

_____

_____

_____

_____

SIMPLE MIND-SET

BE POSITIVE

A positive attitude affects how you experience life and how others experience you and respond to you. It frees up the time and energy that negativity absorbs.

☐ I adopted a more positive attitude today.

What happened differently ☐ at home ☐ at work:

_____

_____

_____

_____

We have a tendency to obscure the forest of simple joys with the trees of problems.

Christiane Collange

Label the forest with simple joys and the tree with problems.

The art of art, the glory of expression and the sunshine of the light of letters, is simplicity.

Walt Whitman

A work of art or literature that is glorious in its simplicity:

_____

_____

_____

_____

_____

SIMPLIFY, THEN ADD LIGHTNESS.

Colin Chapman

I simplified _____ today,

then added this lightness: _____

_____

_____

_____

_____

DATE: ___ / ___ / ___

INSTEAD OF A NEW _____ ,

I WORE MY OLD _____ TO THE EVENT TODAY.

_____

_____

_____

_____

_____

DATE: ___ / ___ / ___

INSTEAD OF A NEW _____ , I DRESSED UP MY OLD

_____ WITH _____ FOR AN EVENT TODAY.

_____

_____

_____

_____

_____

Beware of
all enterprises
that require
new clothes.

Henry David Thoreau

YOU CAN ALWAYS COUNT ON A MURDERER FOR A FANCY PROSE STYLE.

Vladimir Nabokov

Who is the murderer, according to Nabokov?

☐ I was nowhere near the scene of the vile crime.

☐ I was dining at a splendid table alone in a lush garden far distant from the perpetration of the crime.

☐ I am innocent.

The language of truth is simple.

Euripides

Who is telling the truth, according to Euripides?

☐ I was nowhere near the scene of the vile crime.

☐ I was dining at a splendid table alone in a lush garden far distant from the perpetration of the crime.

☐ I am innocent.

DATE: ___/___/___

K.I.S.S.
Shoes

KEEP IT SIMPLE, (STUPID).

Purge your shoes! You need no more than one pair of shoes in the categories listed below. Next to each category, first list the number of pairs of shoes you own. In the next column, write the number after you have purged.

MEN

Sneaker _____ _____

Oxford _____ _____

Boot _____ _____

Sandal _____ _____

Loafer _____ _____

WOMEN

Sneaker _____ _____

Heels _____ _____

Boot _____ _____

Sandal _____ _____

Flats _____ _____

One shoe can change your life.

Cinderella

My _____ changed my life because:

_____

_____

_____

_____

_____

_____

BREVITY IS THE SOUL OF WIT.

William Shakespeare

My best short joke:

_____

_____

_____

I would have written a shorter letter, but I did not have the time.

Blaise Pascal

My shortest written communication today:

_____

_____

_____

Everything will
pass, and the world
will perish but the
Ninth Symphony
will remain.

Mikhail Bakunin

DATE: ___/___/___

THE ONE PIECE OF MUSIC I WILL ALWAYS NEED TO HEAR:

_____

_____

_____

_____

_____

DATE: ___/___/___

THE ONE WORK OF ART I WILL ALWAYS NEED TO SEE:

_____

_____

_____

_____

_____

_____

Gie me ae spark
       O' Nature's fire,
That's a' the learning
       I desire.

Robert Burns

Something I learned from being in nature today:

_____

_____

_____

Earth and sky, woods and fields, lakes and rivers, the mountain and the sea, are excellent schoolmasters, and teach some of us more than we can ever learn from books.

John Lubbock

My schoolmaster today was:

_____

_____

_____

BACK TO BASICS
TOOL KIT:

Pare down your tool collection. Most home repair jobs can be handled with these 10 basic items. Mark the ones you already own.

- ☐ 1-pound hammer
- ☐ rubber mallet
- ☐ cordless drill
- ☐ multi-bit screwdriver
- ☐ adjustable wrench
- ☐ needle-nose pliers
- ☐ utility knife
- ☐ level
- ☐ tape measure
- ☐ safety goggles

A BAD WORKMAN ALWAYS BLAMES HIS TOOLS.

English proverb

I used these basic tools to make a _____ today:

_____

_____

_____

TRULY IT HAS BEEN SAID, THAT TO
A CLEAR EYE THE SMALLEST FACT
IS A WINDOW THROUGH WHICH
THE INFINITE MAY BE SEEN.

Thomas Henry Huxley

A fact I learned today that opened a window for me:

_____

_____

_____

_____

A woodland in full color is awesome as a forest fire . . . but a single tree is like a dancing tongue of flame to warm the heart.

Hal Borland

A small part of nature that warmed my heart today:

_____

_____

_____

_____

_____

WHAT I CHOSE TO OMIT FROM A CONVERSATION TODAY:

_____

_____

_____

_____

_____

_____

WHAT I CHOSE TO OMIT FROM MY WRITING TODAY:

_____

_____

_____

_____

_____

_____

OMISSIONS
ARE NOT
ACCIDENTS.

Marianne Moore

Any intelligent fool can make things bigger. more complex. and more violent. It takes a touch of genius—and a lot of courage to move in the opposite direction.

E. F. Schumacher

Today I simplified _____

by: _____

_____

_____

_____

_____

_____

_____ **I am a genius!**

I hate American simplicity. I glory in the piling up of complications of every sort. If I could pronounce the name James in any different or more elaborate way I should be in favour of doing it.

Henry James

Which name do you prefer?

☐ Muhammad Ali ☐ Cassius Clay

☐ Jay-Z ☐ Shawn Corey Carter

☐ Chance the Rapper ☐ Chancelor Johnathan Bennett

☐ Sting ☐ Gordon Sumner

☐ Whoopi Goldberg ☐ Caryn Elaine Johnson

☐ Lady Gaga ☐ Stefani Joanne Angelina Germanotta

☐ Lorde ☐ Ella Marija Lani Yelich-O'Connor

Simple tips: Dirt

Leave your shoes at the door so that you bring less dirt inside.

○ I now follow this simple rule.

HOUSEKEEPING AIN'T NO JOKE.

Louisa May Alcott

The parts of housekeeping I take seriously:

_____

_____

_____

I SEE NO REASON WHY I SHOULD TICKLE STONES OR WASTE TIME ON POLISHING BRONZE.

Louise Nevelson

I no longer waste time:

☐ wearing shoes that need to be polished

☐ wearing clothes that need to be ironed

☐ preparing gourmet dinners

☐ _____
    other

To gild refined gold, to paint the lily,
To throw a perfume on the violet,
To smooth the ice, or add another hue
Unto the rainbow, or with taper-light
To seek the beauteous eye of heaven to garnish,
Is wasteful and ridiculous excess.

William Shakespeare

Today I gave up this wasteful and ridiculous excess:

_____

_____

_____

_____

_____

THE TRUE
ESSENTIALS OF
A FEAST ARE
ONLY FUN AND
FEED.

Oliver Wendell Holmes, Sr.

DATE: ___ / ___ / ___

FEAST #1 FUN AND FEED:

_____

_____

_____

_____

_____

DATE: ___ / ___ / ___

FEAST #2 FUN AND FEED:

_____

_____

_____

_____

_____

_____

An acre in Middlesex is better than a principality in Utopia.

Lord Macaulay

My simple "acre in Middlesex":

_____

_____

_____

MID PLEASURES AND PALACES THOUGH WE MAY ROAM, BE IT EVER SO HUMBLE, THERE'S NO PLACE LIKE HOME.

John Howard Payne

I have visited _____ ,

_____ ,

and _____ , but there is no place like home.

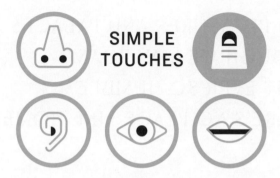

SIMPLE TOUCHES

Maya Angelou

I've learned that every day you should reach out and touch someone. People love a warm hug, or just a friendly pat on the back.

Someone I touched today: _____

Someone who touched me today: _____

DATE: __ / __ / __

Let the rain kiss you.
Let the rain beat upon your
head with silver liquid drops.

Langston Hughes

How the rain felt today:

_____

_____

_____

_____

_____

IF YOU WALK HARD ENOUGH, YOU PROBABLY DON'T NEED ANY OTHER GOD.

Bruce Chatwin

My hard walk today:

_____

_____

_____

_____

_____

DATE: ___/___/___

Fishing is much more than fish. It is the great occasion when we may return to the fine simplicity of our forefathers.

Herbert Hoover

What I did today that brought me closer to the simplicity of my ancestors:

_____

_____

_____

_____

_____

DATE: ___ / ___ / ___

THE FIRST THINGS I WANT TO ACCOMPLISH EVERY DAY:

_____

_____

_____

_____

_____

_____

DATE: ___ / ___ / ___

THE SECOND THINGS I WANT TO ELIMINATE FROM MY DAY:

_____

_____

_____

_____

_____

_____

FIRST THINGS FIRST, SECOND THINGS NEVER.

Shirley Conran

Any nose
May ravage with
impunity a rose.

Robert Browning

Today I ravaged with impunity a _____ :
                                                                flower

FLOWERS.

Those free gifts laid out on

Mother Nature's perfume counter.

Roger McGough

My favorite perfume from nature today:

_____

_____

_____

_____

_____

K.I.S.S.
Electronics

KEEP IT SIMPLE, (STUPID).

List all the electronics you have operating right now:

- _____
- _____
- _____
- _____
- _____
- _____
- _____
- _____

☐ too many   ☐ too few   ☐ just the right number

DATE: ___ / ___ / ___

Almost everything will work again if you unplug it for a few minutes, including you.

Anne Lamott

I unplugged all my electronic devices today for ___ minutes. This is what I accomplished in my offline time:

_____

_____

_____

_____

_____

You can't understand it [fatherhood] until you experience the simple joy of the first time your son points at a seagull and says, "Duck."

Russell Crowe

A simple joy a child brought me today:

_____

_____

_____

_____

_____

DATE: ___/___/___

Behold the child,
    by Nature's kindly law,
Pleased with a rattle,
    tickled with a straw.

Alexander Pope

A simple toy I used to entertain a child today:

_____

_____

_____

_____

_____

ALL THAT
MATTERS
IS LOVE
AND
WORK.

Sigmund Freud

DATE: ___ / ___ / ___

HOW MUCH TIME I DEVOTED TO LOVING TODAY:

_____

_____

_____

_____

_____

_____

DATE: ___ / ___ / ___

HOW MUCH TIME I DEVOTED TO WORKING TODAY:

_____

_____

_____

_____

_____

_____

I do nothing, granted. But I see the hours pass—which is better than trying to fill them.

E. M. Cioran

The "nothing" that filled my hours today:

_____

_____

_____

_____

_____

Life is a matter of passing the time enjoyably. There may be other things in life, but I've been too busy passing my time enjoyably to think very deeply about them.

Peter Cook

How I passed my time enjoyably today:

_____

_____

_____

_____

_____

Simple Gifts

Address the tag
for a simple gift
you gave today:

WAXED LEAF

to:

other

to:

CRAFT
PROJECT

to:

FRESH-PICKED
BERRIES

to:

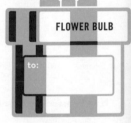

FLOWER BULB

to:

LOVE LETTER

to:

PORTRAIT

to: _____

LUXURY SOAP

to:

I wait for a chance to confer a great favor, and let the small ones slip; but they tell best in the end, I fancy.

Louisa May Alcott

A small favor conferred on me today:

_____

_____

_____

_____

_____

DATE: __ / __ / __

SIMPLICITY IS A STATE OF MIND.

Charles Wagner

I simplified my day by:

_____

_____

_____

_____

_____

To see a world in a grain of sand
And a heaven in a wild flower
Hold infinity in the palm of your hand
And eternity in an hour.

William Blake

This small thing opened my mind to something great today:

DATE: ___ / ___ / ___

FURNITURE I NEED:

_____

_____

FURNITURE THAT IS CONVENIENT:

_____

_____

DATE: ___ / ___ / ___

FURNITURE THAT IS A NEEDLESS LUXURY:

_____

_____

WHAT I WILL DO WITH MY NEEDLESS FURNITURE:

_____

_____

Thus first necessity
invented stools,

Convenience
next suggested
elbow-chairs,

And luxury
the accomplished
sofa last.

William Cowper

When all at once I saw a crowd,

A host of golden daffodils;

. . . A poet could not but be gay,

In such a jocund company:

I gazed—and gazed—but little thought

What wealth to me the show had brought.

William Wordsworth

This simple sight today brought me a wealth of joy:

_____

_____

_____

Deprivation is for me what daffodils were for Wordsworth.

Philip Larkin

_____ is for me what daffodils were for Wordsworth.

Simple tips: Morning

Get up an hour earlier and make it your time to do what you want.

Today I got up an hour earlier and used the time to:

○ organize my day

○ meditate

○ exercise

○ read

○ write in my journal

○ give thanks

○ soak in the tub

○ _____
      other

You will accomplish as much in one morning hour as in two evening hours.

Arnold Bennett

What I accomplished by rising one hour early today:

_____

_____

_____

_____

SIMPLICITY IS NATURE'S FIRST STEP, AND THE LAST OF ART.

Philip James Bailey

Draw an animal without lifting your pencil.

Art should simplify. That is very nearly the whole of the higher artistic process; finding what conventions of form and what detail one can do without and yet preserve the spirit of the whole.

Willa Cather

With a single line, draw a self-portrait that preserves your spirit.

THE WORLD IS TOO
MUCH WITH US;
LATE AND SOON,

GETTING AND
SPENDING, WE
LAY WASTE OUR
POWERS;–

LITTLE WE SEE IN
NATURE THAT IS
OURS.

William Wordsworth

DATE: ___ /___ /___

INSTEAD OF BUYING SOMETHING TODAY, I FOUND THIS IN NATURE:

_____

_____

_____

_____

_____

_____

DATE: ___ /___ /___

**INSTEAD OF SPENDING MONEY ON ENTERTAINMENT TODAY,
I DID THIS OUTDOORS:**

_____

_____

_____

_____

_____

_____

DATE: ___/___/___

IN THE UNIVERSE GREAT ACTS ARE MADE UP OF SMALL DEEDS.

Lao-tzu

Small deeds that made up a great act today:

_____

_____

_____

_____

_____

When you rise in the morning, form a resolution to make the day a happy one to a fellow-creature.

Sydney Smith

This morning I resolved to make the day a happy one for a fellow creature by:

_____

_____

_____

_____

_____

SIMPLE
MIND-SET

PRIORITIZE

To simplify the demands of work and home, make a list of
your five goals for the day, numbering from the most (#1)
to the least important. Start with #1, so that what is most
critical will always get done. Then you can reevaluate
the rest of your list.

What I must do at work today:

_____

_____

_____

_____

_____

There was no need to do any housework at all. After the first four years the dirt doesn't get any worse.

Quentin Crisp

My high-priority goals for housework today:

_____

_____

_____

_____

_____

A morning-glory at my window
satisfies me more than
the metaphysics of books.

Walt Whitman

This satisfied me more than reading a book today:

_____

_____

_____

_____

_____

Human subtlety . . . will never devise an invention more beautiful, more simple or more direct than does nature, because in her inventions nothing is lacking, and nothing is superfluous.

Leonardo da Vinci

What I appreciated about nature today:

_____

_____

_____

_____

_____

DATE: ___/___/___

FILL THIS BACKPACK
WITH BELONGINGS
THAT REFLECT YOU:

DATE: ___/___/___

CIRCLE ONE ITEM IN YOUR
BACKPACK YOU WOULD SACRIFICE
FOR SOMETHING NEW.

I TRAVELED FOR THE WHOLE
YEAR WITH NOTHING BUT ONE
BACKPACK AND I HAD A RULE:
WHEN ANYTHING NEW CAME
INTO MY BACKPACK, SOMETHING
HAD TO GO. I BEGAN CREATING
A LIFE THAT REALLY LOOKED LIKE
ME, RATHER THAN LOOKING LIKE
EVERYTHING I HAD ACCUMULATED
UP UNTIL THAT POINT.

Elizabeth Gilbert

Blessed are they who see beautiful things in humble places where other people see nothing.

Camille Pissarro

Something beautiful I saw in a humble place today:

_____

_____

_____

_____

_____

DATE: ___/___/___

If the sight of the blue skies fills you with joy,
if a blade of grass springing up in the fields has power to
move you, if the simple things of nature have a message
that you understand, rejoice, for your soul is alive.

Eleonora Duse

A simple thing in nature that made my soul alive today:

_____

_____

_____

_____

_____

DATE: __/__/__

KEEP IT SIMPLE, (STUPID).

K.I.S.S.
Desserts

This simple recipe for One-Ingredient Banana Ice Cream got 4 stars (out of 5) in *The New York Times:*

Peel 4 bananas and cut them into 2- to 3-inch chunks. Freeze them in a plastic bag for at least 6 hours, then blend the frozen chunks in a blender or food processor until the mixture is smooth. Serve immediately as soft-serve ice cream.

☐ Today I made this simple dessert, which tasted so sophisticated.

Cooking well doesn't mean cooking fancy.

Julia Child

An un-fancy dessert I created today: _____

_____

_____

_____

_____

IT SEEMS THAT PERFECTION IS
ATTAINED NOT WHEN THERE IS
NOTHING MORE TO ADD, BUT WHEN
THERE IS NOTHING MORE TO REMOVE.

Antoine de Saint-Exupéry

There is nothing more to remove from my _____.

_____

_____

_____

_____

_____

Simplicity of life, even the barest, is not a misery, but the very foundation of refinement; a sanded floor and whitewashed walls and the green trees, and flowery meads, and living waters outside.

William Morris

Describe your ideal of a simple dwelling:

_____

_____

_____

_____

_____

OUT OF
INTENSE
COMPLEXITIES
INTENSE
SIMPLICITIES
EMERGE.

Winston Churchill

DATE: ___ / ___ / ___

A SIMPLE SOLUTION TO AN INTENSELY COMPLEX PROBLEM AT WORK TODAY:

_____

_____

_____

_____

_____

_____

DATE: ___ / ___ / ___

A SIMPLE SOLUTION TO AN INTENSELY COMPLEX PROBLEM AT HOME TODAY:

_____

_____

_____

_____

_____

_____

IT WAS A DELIGHTFUL VISIT; –PERFECT, IN BEING MUCH TOO SHORT.

Jane Austen

I had a delightful visit today with _____

_____

that lasted only _____.

I had three chairs in my house; one for solitude, two for friendship, three for society.

Henry David Thoreau

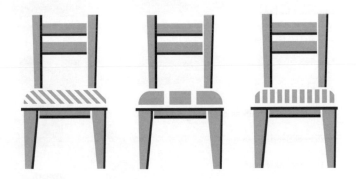

Chair #1 for Me

Chair #1 and #2 for Me and _____.

Chair #1 and #2 and #3 for Me and _____ **and** _____.

BACK TO BASICS
OVER-THE-COUNTER MEDICINES:

To simplify your medicine cabinet, first discard any medicines that have expired. Then make sure that you have the basics. The Mayo Clinic's suggested first-aid kit includes these 10 over-the-counter medications. Mark the ones you already have:

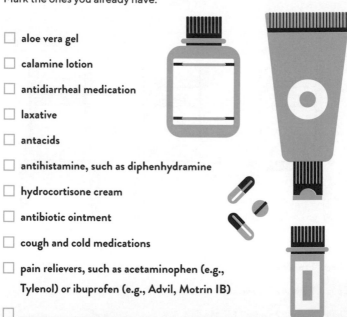

- ☐ aloe vera gel
- ☐ calamine lotion
- ☐ antidiarrheal medication
- ☐ laxative
- ☐ antacids
- ☐ antihistamine, such as diphenhydramine
- ☐ hydrocortisone cream
- ☐ antibiotic ointment
- ☐ cough and cold medications
- ☐ pain relievers, such as acetaminophen (e.g., Tylenol) or ibuprofen (e.g., Advil, Motrin IB)
- ☐ _____
  personal needs

Natural forces within us are the true healers of disease.

Hippocrates

My favorite home remedy is:

_____

_____

_____

Hospitality consists in a little fire, a little food, and an immense quiet.

Ralph Waldo Emerson

My idea of hospitality consists of:

_____

_____

_____

_____

_____

But every house where Love abides
And Friendship is a guest,
Is surely home, and home, sweet home,
For there the heart can rest.

Henry Van Dyke

How I make my house "home, sweet home":

_____

_____

_____

_____

DATE: ___ /___ /___

A GREAT SIMPLE TRUTH I DISCOVERED TODAY:

_____

_____

_____

_____

_____

_____

DATE: ___ /___ /___

A SIMPLE, STRAIGHTFORWARD PERSON I KNOW TO BE GREAT:

_____

_____

_____

_____

_____

_____

The greatest truths
are the simplest,
and so are
the greatest men.

J. C. and A. W. Hare

EXPECT NOTHING. LIVE FRUGALLY ON SURPRISE.

Alice Walker

What happily surprised me today:

_____

_____

_____

_____

_____

DATE: __ / __ / __

When one's expectations are reduced to zero, one really appreciates everything one does have.

Stephen Hawking

Something I have that I appreciated today:

_____

_____

_____

_____

_____

Simple tips: Bills

Sign up for electronic billing for recurring charges, which will eliminate paper clutter. Be sure to store a pdf of the bill every month in an electronic folder with the date.

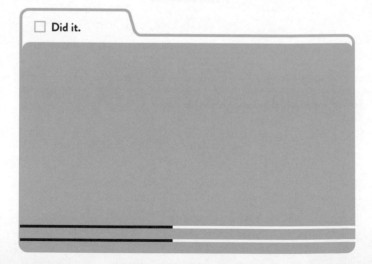

☐ Did it.

It's not the load that weighs you down, it's how you carry it.

C. S. Lewis, attributed

Paying bills electronically relieved me of:

_____

_____

_____

_____

I will arise and go now, and go to Innisfree,
And a small cabin build there, of clay and wattles made;
Nine bean-rows will I have there, a hive for the honey-bee,
And live alone in the bee-loud glade.

William Butler Yeats

Describe your happy place:

_____

_____

_____

_____

_____

AH! THERE IS NOTHING LIKE STAYING AT HOME, FOR REAL COMFORT.

Jane Austen

Today I just stayed home. What a pleasure:

_____

_____

_____

_____

_____

Reinvent new
combinations of what
you already own.
Improvise. Become
more creative.
Not because you have
to, but because you
want to.

Karl Lagerfeld

DATE: __/__/__

THIS IS MY FAVORITE PARTY OUTFIT:

HOW I VARY MY FAVORITE PARTY OUTFIT:

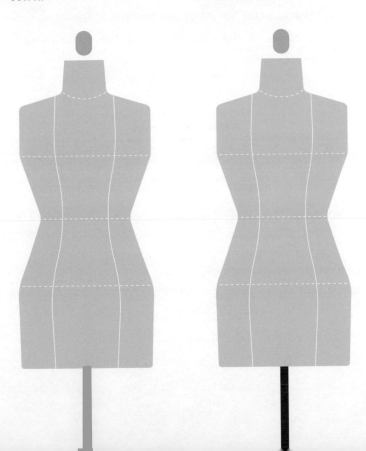

DATE: ___/___/___

I will be as harsh as truth and as uncompromising as justice. On this subject I do not wish to think, or speak, or write, with moderation.

William Lloyd Garrison

I will not be moderate on this subject: _____

_____

_____

_____

_____

_____

Extremism in the defense of liberty is no vice. Moderation in the pursuit of justice is no virtue.

Barry M. Goldwater

Extremism in the defense of _____ is a virtue.

_____

_____

_____

_____

_____

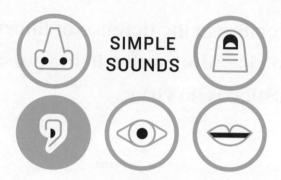

SIMPLE
SOUNDS

Alan Watts | The sound of rain needs no translation.

The sound of _____ needs no translation.

THE WREN AND THE NIGHTINGALE
SOUND NOTHING ALIKE, BUT THINK
HOW DULL THE WORLD WOULD BE
WITHOUT THE SONGS OF BOTH BIRDS.

Kirby Larson

The simple sounds of these birds brighten my world:

Simplicity is not so simple to attain.

Nassim Nicholas Taleb

I did this hard work today to simplify a future chore:

_____

_____

_____

_____

_____

Simplicity—the art of maximizing the amount of work not done— is essential.

Principles behind the Agile Manifesto (2001)

Today I maximized the amount of work not done by:

☐ delegating

☐ partnering

☐ eliminating redundancies

☐ eliminating nonessentials

☐ _____
       other

DATE: ___/___/___

A SMILE AND KINDNESS I RECEIVED THAT WON MY HEART TODAY:

_____

_____

_____

_____

_____

_____

DATE: ___/___/___

A SMALL OBLIGATION I FULFILLED THAT PRESERVED MY HEART TODAY:

_____

_____

_____

_____

_____

_____

Life is made up, not of
great sacrifices or duties,
but of little things, in which
smiles and kindness, and small
obligations . . . win and
preserve the heart.

Sir Humphry Davy

DATE: ___/___/___

"I PLAY FOR SEASONS; NOT ETERNITIES!" SAYS NATURE.

George Meredith

Today I focused on this moment:

_____

_____

_____

_____

_____

DATE: ___/___/___

[Take] short views of human life—not further than dinner or tea.

Sydney Smith

My short-term goal today:

_____

_____

_____

_____

K.I.S.S.
Exercise

Eliminate all exercise equipment and start walking. According to many physicians, a 30-minute walk each day provides all the aerobic exercise you need to maintain health.

☐ Today I got rid of all my exercise equipment and started a program of walking every day.

Walking is the best possible exercise.

Thomas Jefferson

☐ If walking was good enough for a Founding Father, it is good enough for me.

DATE: __/__/__

THE LESS WE INDULGE OUR PLEASURES THE MORE WE ENJOY THEM.

Juvenal

A rare pleasure I enjoyed today:

_____

_____

_____

_____

_____

Let us not take it for granted that life exists more fully in what is commonly thought big than in what is commonly thought small.

Virginia Woolf

A "small" pleasure I enjoyed today:

_____

_____

_____

_____

_____

O HOLY
SIMPLICITY!

John Huss

DATE: ___ / ___ / ___

HOW I SIMPLIFIED MY CLOSET TODAY (HALLELUJAH!):

_____

_____

_____

_____

_____

_____

DATE: ___ / ___ / ___

HOW I SIMPLIFIED MY COMMUTE TODAY (JOY!):

_____

_____

_____

_____

_____

HOW CAN YOU GOVERN
A COUNTRY WHICH HAS
246 VARIETIES OF CHEESE?

Charles de Gaulle

Today I pruned my collection of

☐ belts

☐ scarves

☐ T-shirts

☐ ties

☐ books

☐ _____
       other

The tragedy of English cooking is that "plain" cooking cannot be entrusted to "plain" cooks.

Countess Morphy

I spice up my plain cooking by:

_____

_____

_____

_____

Simple Gifts

Address the tag
for a simple gift
you gave today:

SPECIAL ROCK

to:

DANCE

to:

other

to:

SCENTED
CANDLE

to:

PHOTOGRAPH

to:

COFFEE WITH
FOAM HEART

to:

PRESSED FLOWER

to: _____

COZY BLANKET

to:

DATE: __ / __ / __

Every gift, though it be small, is in reality great if given with affection.

Pindar

This small gift was given to me today by my beloved friend:

_____

_____

_____

_____

_____

Beauty of style and harmony and grace and good rhythm depend on simplicity.

Plato

A beautiful object by Plato's standards:

_____

_____

_____

_____

_____

Style is the man himself.

Georges-Louis Leclerc, Comte de Buffon

A person whose style I admire:

_____

_____

_____

_____

_____

HOW I ACTED PLAINLY AND SIMPLY TODAY:

_____

_____

_____

_____

_____

_____

HOW I REDUCED MY SELFISHNESS AND DESIRES TODAY:

_____

_____

_____

_____

_____

_____

MANIFEST PLAINNESS, EMBRACE SIMPLICITY, REDUCE SELFISHNESS, HAVE FEW DESIRES.

Lao-tzu

Soup not only warms you and is easy to swallow and to digest, it also creates the illusion in the back of your mind that Mother is there.

Marlene Dietrich

This simple thing creates the illusion that Mother is here:

_____

_____

_____

_____

_____

There was something immensely comforting,
I found, about a crumpet—so comforting that
I've never forgotten about them and have even
learned to make them myself against those
times when I have no other source of supply.

Peg Bracken

A simple food that brought me comfort today:

_____

_____

_____

_____

Simple tips:
Buy in Bulk

For products you use regularly, find a retailer where you can set up a continuing order.

PRODUCT	RETAILER	RENEWAL RATE

Weekend planning is a prime time to apply the Deathbed Priority Test: On your deathbed, will you wish you had spent more prime weekend hours grocery shopping or walking in the woods with your kids?

Hal Borland

Purchasing by automatic renewal gave me more time today to do this:

_____

_____

_____

_____

WITH TRUE FRIENDS EVEN WATER DRUNK TOGETHER IS SWEET ENOUGH.

Proverb

With _____,

even water drunk together is sweet.

One friend in a lifetime is much; two are many, three are hardly possible.

Henry Brooks Adams

My one friend of a lifetime: _____

My second friend of a lifetime: _____

The more we look, the more we see
How many precious things are free,
The heart will find more than the eye
Of things we do not need to buy.

John Martin

DATE: ___ / ___ / ___

SOMETHING PRECIOUS I FOUND FOR FREE TODAY:

_____

_____

_____

_____

_____

_____

DATE: ___ / ___ / ___

SOMETHING PRECIOUS I DID NOT NEED TO BUY TODAY:

_____

_____

_____

_____

_____

_____

When a thought is too weak to be expressed simply, it should be rejected.

Luc, Marquis de Vauvenargues

Today my idea was rejected because no one understood it. Here I explain it more simply:

_____

_____

_____

_____

_____

The necessity of making things plain to uninstructed people was one of the very best means of clearing up the obscure corners in one's own mind.

Thomas Henry Huxley

Today I explained this complicated idea simply and now understand it better myself:

_____

_____

_____

_____

_____

SIMPLE
MIND-SET

CULTIVATE
INNER RESOURCES

Notice the simple activities—reading, gardening, taking walks, bird-watching, stitching, cooking, listening to music— that bring you pleasure. To indulge them regularly is not an indulgence. You are building reserves that you can count on to fill your life when you need them.

Simple activities that bring me pleasure:

_____

_____

_____

_____

A mind lively and at ease, can do with seeing nothing, and can see nothing that does not answer.

Jane Austen

How I happily entertained myself alone today:

_____

_____

_____

_____

The Lord prefers common-looking people. That is why he makes so many of them.

Abraham Lincoln

_____, a common-looking person, is beautiful to me

because: _____

_____

_____

_____

_____

_____

BEAUTY IS IN THE EYE OF THE BEHOLDER.

Margaret Wolfe Hungerford

_____, a common-looking object, is beautiful to me

because: _____

_____

_____

_____

_____

_____

DATE: ___ / ___ / ___

THE WAYS MY HOUSE FOLLOWS THE TWO GREAT RULES FOR DESIGN:

_____

_____

_____

_____

_____

_____

DATE: ___ / ___ / ___

A BUILDING I ADMIRE THAT FOLLOWS THE TWO GREAT RULES FOR DESIGN:

_____

_____

_____

_____

_____

_____

THE TWO GREAT RULES FOR DESIGN ARE THESE:

1st, that there should be no features about a building that are not necessary for convenience, construction, or propriety;

2nd, that all ornament should consist of the essential construction of the building.

Augustus Welby Pugin

It is always the simple that produces the marvelous.

Amelia Barr

Something simple today that produced a marvelous result:

_____

_____

_____

_____

_____

A man is simple when his chief care
is the wish to be what he ought to be,
that is honestly and naturally human.

Charles Wagner

A simple person I know, honest and natural:

_____

_____

_____

_____

DATE: __/__/__

K.I.S.S.
Packing for Travel

Check off these recommendations
for simpler packing next time you travel:

☐ Use a carry-on suitcase.

☐ Limit your clothing to two
colors that mix and match.

☐ Make a list and mark each
item as you pack it.

DATE: ___/___/___

Simplicity is making the journey of this life with just baggage enough.

Charles Dudley Warner

When you return home from a trip, sort the items you unpack into two piles: what I used and what I didn't use. Next time bring only what you used.

What I used _____

_____

What I didn't use _____

_____

DATE: __/__/__

STYLE IS CHARACTER.

Joan Didion

How I would characterize my style today:

_____

_____

_____

_____

_____

_____

_____

Style is not neutral; it gives moral directions.

Martin Amis

I hope that adopting a simple style will lead me to be more:

- ☐ honest

- ☐ charitable

- ☐ faithful

- ☐ kind

- ☐ tolerant

- ☐ modest

- ☐ _____
  other

Fear less, hope more;
eat less, chew more; whine
less, breathe more; talk less,
say more; hate less, love more;
and all good things
will be yours.

Swedish proverb

DATE: ___ / ___ / ___

HOW I MANAGED TO FEAR, EAT, WHINE, TALK, AND HATE LESS TODAY:

_____

_____

_____

_____

_____

_____

DATE: ___ / ___ / ___

HOW I MANAGED TO HOPE, CHEW, BREATHE, SAY, AND LOVE MORE TODAY:

_____

_____

_____

_____

_____

_____

How far that little candle
throws its beams!
So shines a good deed in
a naughty world.

William Shakespeare

A good deed I did today:

_____

_____

_____

_____

_____

_____

To be really great in little things, to be truly noble and heroic in the insipid details of everyday life, is a virtue so rare as to be worthy of canonization.

Harriet Beecher Stowe

I consider _____ the Saint of Details of Everyday Life

because: _____

_____

_____

_____

_____

BACK TO BASICS
GARDEN TOOLS:

Prune your gardening kit. With these 10 tools, you can plant and tend a simple Garden of Eden. Mark the ones you already own.

- ☐ pruning shears
- ☐ loppers
- ☐ hand trowel
- ☐ spade
- ☐ rake
- ☐ hoe
- ☐ garden fork
- ☐ watering can
- ☐ garden hose with adjustable nozzle
- ☐ wheelbarrow

DATE: ___ / ___ / ___

To own a bit of ground, to scratch it
with a hoe, to plant seeds and watch
their renewal of life—this is the
commonest delight.

Charles Dudley Warner

What I ☐ planted ☐ grew ☐ harvested today:

_____

_____

_____

TOO BEAUTIFUL FOR OUR EARS, AND FAR TOO MANY NOTES, DEAR MOZART.

Joseph II, Holy Roman emperor

A musical work too rich for my taste:

_____

_____

_____

_____

Simplicity is the final achievement. After one has played a vast quantity of notes and more notes, it is simplicity that emerges as the crowning reward of art.

Frédéric Chopin

A simple melody I like to hum:

_____

_____

_____

_____

_____

DATE: ___ / ___ / ___

WHAT I CAN LEARN FROM MOTHER INDIA ABOUT EATING SIMPLY:

_____

_____

_____

_____

_____

_____

DATE: ___ / ___ / ___

WHAT I CAN LEARN FROM MOTHER INDIA ABOUT WHAT IS ESSENTIAL:

_____

_____

_____

_____

_____

_____

In a country as hot as India, a person really requires very few essentials in order to live: one vegetarian meal a day, rice bread, vegetables and lentils, two pieces of clothing to wear, a mat, a blanket, a lota, a water container. . . . Mother India is a great teacher of simplicity.

Gaura Devi

We adore chaos because we love to produce order.

M. C. Escher

Today I put this chaos in order:

_____

_____

_____

_____

_____

Art has something to do with the achievement of stillness in the midst of chaos.

Saul Bellow

How I achieved stillness in the midst of chaos today:

_____

_____

_____

_____

_____

Simple tips:
E-mail

Set up two e-mail addresses: one for your personal/
business communications and the other for subscriptions.
This will make it easier for you to reply to people more
quickly and read subscriptions or unsubscribe at
your leisure.

☐ Did it.

Nobody sees a flower really;
it is so small. We haven't time,
and to see takes time—like to
have a friend takes time.

Georgia O'Keeffe

Spend the time to really
see a flower today.
Draw it here:

We ascribe beauty to that which is simple; which has no superfluous parts; which exactly answers its end; which stands related to all things; which is the mean of many extremes.

Ralph Waldo Emerson

Something with no superfluous parts, which I think is beautiful:

_____

_____

_____

_____

_____

There is one order of beauty which seems made to turn heads. It is a beauty like that of kittens, or very small downy ducks making gently rippling noises with their soft bills, or babies just beginning to toddle.

George Eliot

An order of beauty that made my head turn today:

_____

_____

_____

_____

NEITHER
ABSTINENCE
NOR EXCESS
EVER RENDERS
MAN HAPPY.

Voltaire

DATE: ___ / ___ / ___

ABSTAINING COMPLETELY FROM THIS MADE ME UNHAPPY TODAY:

_____

_____

_____

_____

_____

_____

DATE: ___ / ___ / ___

INDULGING EXCESSIVELY IN THIS MADE ME UNHAPPY TODAY:

_____

_____

_____

_____

_____

_____

DATE: __ / __ / __

Every day we should hear at least
one little song, read one good poem,
see one exquisite picture, and,
if possible, speak a few sensible words.

Johann Wolfgang von Goethe

These simple pleasures were enough for today:

☐ one little song _____

☐ one good poem _____

☐ one exquisite picture _____

☐ these few sensible words _____

It does not matter whether one paints a picture, writes a poem, or carves a statue—simplicity is the mark of a master-hand.

Elsie de Wolfe

Master-hands I admire:

painter _____

poet _____

sculptor _____

SIMPLE SCENTS

Walter Hagen	You're only here for a short visit. Don't hurry, don't worry. And be sure to smell the flowers along the way.

I stopped and smelled these "flowers" today:

_____

_____

_____

Nothing is more memorable than a smell. One scent can be unexpected, momentary, and fleeting, yet conjure up a childhood summer beside a lake in the mountains.

Diane Ackerman

The scent of _____ today brought me back to:

_____

_____

_____

DATE: ___ / ___ / ___

Everybody gets so much information all day long that they lose their common sense.

Gertrude Stein

How I turned off the flow of information today:

_____

_____

_____

_____

_____

DATE: __ / __ / __

More important than learning how to recall things is finding ways to forget things that are cluttering the mind.

Eric Butterworth

How I forget things that clutter my mind:
- ☐ listen to music
- ☐ meditate
- ☐ make a list
- ☐ watch a show
- ☐ sleep
- ☐ exercise
- ☐ _____
  other

DESCRIBE ONE ELEMENT OF A BUILDING THAT STRUCK YOU AS POETIC TODAY:

_____

_____

_____

_____

_____

_____

DRAW A SINGLE TREE THAT STRUCK YOU AS POETIC TODAY:

THE POETRY OF
ART IS IN BEHOLDING
THE SINGLE TOWER;
THE POETRY OF NATURE
IN SEEING THE SINGLE
TREE.

Gilbert K. Chesterton

DATE: ___/___/___

IN THE END, WHAT AFFECT YOUR LIFE MOST DEEPLY ARE THINGS TOO SIMPLE TO TALK ABOUT.

Nell Blaine

Something simple that has affected my life deeply:

_____

_____

_____

_____

_____

DATE: ___/___/___

The thing that is important is the thing that is not seen.

Antoine de Saint-Exupéry

Something unseen that affected my life today:

_____

_____

_____

_____

_____

KEEP IT SIMPLE, (STUPID).

K.I.S.S.
Organize

Use expert organizer Julie Morgenstern's S.P.A.C.E. formula to make the task of organizing manageable, methodical, and rewarding. Do every one of the steps and, most important, do them in order.

Today I S.P.A.C.E.d my closet:

☐ S = Sort

☐ P = Purge

☐ A = Assign a home

☐ C = Containerize

☐ E = Equalize (i.e., maintain the system)

First organize your physical spaces, especially in the hot spots: kitchen, front entry, bathroom, living room, making sure everything has a really simple, well-labeled home.

Julie Morgenstern

Today I S.P.A.C.E.d this hot spot in my home:

_____

Saying nothing . . .
sometimes says the most.

Emily Dickinson

Someone I comforted by listening today:

_____

_____

_____

_____

DATE: ___ / ___ / ___

LISTEN TO SILENCE.
IT HAS SO MUCH TO SAY.

Rumi

What I heard in the silence of nature today:

_____

_____

_____

_____

_____

All the great things are simple,
and many can be expressed
in a single word:

FREEDOM,

JUSTICE,

HONOR,

DUTY,

MERCY,

HOPE.

Winston Churchill

DATE: ___/___/___

A GREAT-BUT-SIMPLE THING I DID FOR ☐ **FREEDOM** ☐ **JUSTICE**
☐ **HONOR TODAY:**

_____

_____

_____

_____

_____

_____

DATE: ___/___/___

A GREAT-BUT-SIMPLE THING I DID FOR ☐ **DUTY** ☐ **MERCY** ☐ **HOPE TODAY:**

_____

_____

_____

_____

_____

_____

A hot bath! How exquisite a vespertine pleasure, how luxurious, fervid and flagrant a consolation for the rigours, the austerities, the renunciations of the day.

Rose Macaulay

An exquisite but simple vespertine pleasure I had today:

_____

_____

_____

_____

_____

DATE: __ / __ / __

How simple and frugal a thing is happiness: a glass of wine, a roast chestnut, a wretched little brazier, the sound of the sea.

Nikos Kazantzakis

Today my happiness was simply this:

_____

_____

_____

_____

Simple Gifts

Address the tag for a simple gift you gave today:

POTPOURRI

to:

BREAKFAST IN BED

to:

other

to:

POPCORN AND A MOVIE

to:

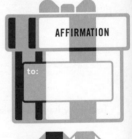

AFFIRMATION

to:

PICNIC

to:

VISIT TO HEAR A BEAUTIFUL SOUND

to: _____

SILLY SOCKS

to:

The best things come in small packages.

Proverb

Today I received the best gift in a "small package":

_____

_____

_____

_____

_____

Moderation multiplies pleasures, and increases pleasure.

Democritus

Today I ate_____, which was not-too-hot, not-too-cold, but just right—yum!

ENOUGH IS AS GOOD AS A FEAST.

John Heywood

Enough _____ was as good as a feast today.

DATE: ___ / ___ / ___

THIS KITCHEN ITEM IS A PERFECT EXAMPLE OF FORM FOLLOWING FUNCTION:

_____

_____

_____

_____

_____

DATE: ___ / ___ / ___

THIS BATHROOM ITEM IS A PERFECT EXAMPLE OF FORM FOLLOWING FUNCTION:

_____

_____

_____

_____

_____

FORM

FOLLOWS

FUNCTION.

Louis H. Sullivan

If you cannot get what you want, common sense suggests that you should put your mind to wanting what you can get.

Patricia Wentworth

Something I no longer covet because I can't have it:

_____

_____

Something I want because I can have it:

_____

_____

IT IS FAR BETTER TO APPRECIATE AND NOT TO POSSESS, THAN TO POSSESS AND NOT TO APPRECIATE.

Lilian Whiting

Something I appreciate, though I cannot possess it:

_____

_____

_____

_____

_____

Simple tips:
Handbag or Tote

Always carry the minimum you will need. Take everything out of your handbag or tote. Circle everything you have:

LOOSE CHANGE

Candy or Gum Wrappers

HAND SANITIZER

brush

KEYS

COMB

mirror

USED TISSUES

COMPUTER CORDS

Lipstick

CELLPHONE

WALLET

CREDIT CARDS

OLD RECEIPTS

PENS AND/ OR PENCILS

_____
other

Put back into your bag
the minimum you will need.
Fill small pouches with similar
items, such as make-up, pens
and pencils, and computer cords.

I WANT DEATH TO FIND ME PLANTING MY CABBAGES.

Michel de Montaigne

My happy place in nature:

_____

_____

_____

_____

All gardening is landscape painting.

Alexander Pope

Draw your ☐ indoor
☐ outdoor
landscape painting.

I STILL HAVE
THE BEST COMFORTS
OF LIFE—BOOKS AND
FRIENDSHIPS—AND I
TRUST NEVER TO LOSE
MY RELISH FOR EITHER.

Mary Russell Mitford

DATE: ___/___/___

BOOKS THAT GIVE ME COMFORT:

_____

_____

_____

_____

_____

_____

DATE: ___/___/___

FRIENDS WHO GIVE ME COMFORT:

_____

_____

_____

_____

_____

_____

Keeping my hands busy helps my mind find stillness.

Marie Kondo

How I kept my hands busy as I sat peacefully today:

_____

_____

_____

_____

_____

We have to become as simple and as wordless as the growing corn or the falling rain. We must just be.

Etty Hillesum

How I was able to just be today:

_____

_____

_____

_____

_____

SIMPLE MIND-SET

ALLOW YOURSELF TO BE LESS THAN PERFECT

Do not sacrifice time, effort, and satisfaction trying to achieve perfection in every area of your life. The best, wrote Voltaire, is "the enemy of the good."

Something I did today that was less than perfect but perfectly good:

_____

_____

_____

_____

THERE IS A CRACK IN EVERYTHING THAT'S HOW THE LIGHT GETS IN.

Leonard Cohen

An imperfection in something I did today:

_____

The light that got in:

_____

We ourselves feel that what we are doing is just a drop in the ocean. But if that drop was not in the ocean, I think the ocean would be less because of that missing drop.

Mother Teresa

A little drop of kindness I contributed today:

_____

_____

_____

_____

_____

I DREAM OF BIG THINGS.
I WORK FOR THE SMALL THINGS.

Kevin Costner

Something small I worked on today, which I hope will develop into my big dream:

_____

_____

_____

_____

_____

DATE: ___/___/___

I REALIZED THAT THIS WAS UNNECESSARY FOR MY WORK TODAY:

_____

_____

_____

_____

_____

_____

DATE: ___/___/___

WHEN I ELIMINATED THE UNNECESSARY FROM MY WORK TODAY, I DISCOVERED THIS:

_____

_____

_____

_____

_____

_____

THE ABILITY
TO SIMPLIFY MEANS
TO ELIMINATE THE
UNNECESSARY SO
THAT THE NECESSARY
MAY SPEAK.

Hans Hofmann

JOY IS NOT IN THINGS; IT IS IN US.

Richard Wagner

Joy rose inside me today when _____

_____

_____

_____

_____

_____

*Happiness depends, as
Nature shows,
Less on exterior things than
most suppose.*

William Cowper

A thought, feeling, memory, or idea that brought me happiness today:

_____

_____

_____

_____

_____

DATE: ___/___/___

K.I.S.S.
Single-Task

Do one thing at a time, instead of trying to do many things simultaneously.

Today, I accomplished this:

_____

Then I went on to do this:

_____

If you chase two rabbits, you will catch neither one.

Russian proverb

The one rabbit I chased and caught today: _____

_____

_____

If we could see the miracle of a single flower clearly, our whole life would change.

Buddha

The miracle I observed in a single flower today:

_____

_____

_____

_____

_____

DATE: __/__/__

*Flowers always make people better,
happier, and more helpful; they are
sunshine, food, and medicine to
the soul.*

Luther Burbank

How flowers made me feel today:

_____

_____

_____

_____

_____

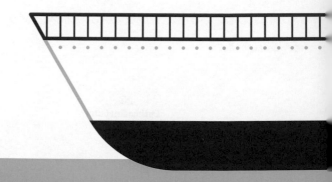

Let your boat of life be light, packed with only what you need—a homely home and simple pleasures, one or two friends, worth the name, someone to love and someone to love you, a cat, a dog, and a pipe or two, enough to eat and enough to wear, and a little more than enough to drink; for thirst is a dangerous thing.

Jerome K. Jerome

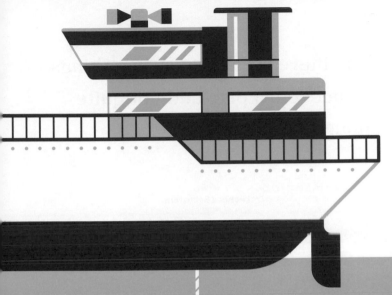

DATE: __/__/__

ADD THE POSSESSIONS
YOU WANT IN YOUR
BOAT OF LIFE.

DATE: __/__/__

DRAW AND LABEL THE PEOPLE AND PETS YOU WANT IN YOUR BOAT OF LIFE.

To achieve great things, two things are needed: a plan and not quite enough time.

Leonard Bernstein

Today I had to simplify my plan because I thought there wasn't enough time, BUT it worked out fine:

_____

_____

_____

_____

_____

It has taken me years of struggle, hard work, and research to learn to make one simple gesture.

Isadora Duncan

Today I achieved my goal—which looks simple—after anything-but-simple hard work:

_____

_____

_____

_____

_____

BACK TO BASICS
SPICES:

Trash the dusty jars of stale spices in the back of your cabinet. Stock it instead with the two true basics—salt (kosher) and pepper (black peppercorns)—and 10 primary spices that you will use often to flavor sweet and savory dishes. Mark the spices you already have.

- [ ] bay leaves
- [ ] ground cinnamon
- [ ] ground cumin
- [ ] curry powder
- [ ] garlic powder
- [ ] ground ginger
- [ ] dried oregano
- [ ] sweet paprika
- [ ] red pepper flakes
- [ ] dried thyme

OF ALL SMELLS, BREAD;
OF ALL TASTES, SALT.

George Herbert

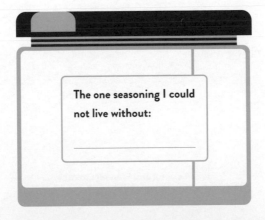

The one seasoning I could
not live without:

ALL YOU NEED IS LOVE.

John Lennon and Paul McCartney

DATE: ___ / ___ / ___

RATE YOUR LIFE TODAY FROM "OVERLY COMPLICATED" TO "PERFECTLY SIMPLE" BY MARKING YOUR PLACE ON THIS METER.

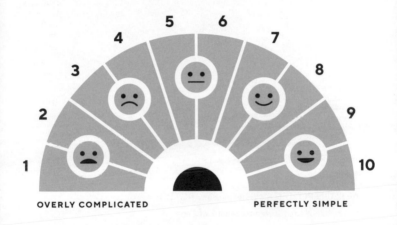

OVERLY COMPLICATED   PERFECTLY SIMPLE

DATE: ___ / ___ / ___

COMPARE THIS WITH THE METER YOU MARKED AT THE BEGINNING OF THE BOOK. WHAT DO YOU THINK?

_____

_____

_____

Published in the United States by Clarkson Potter/
Publishers, an imprint of Random House, a division
of Penguin Random House LLC, New York.
clarksonpotter.com

CLARKSON POTTER is a trademark and POTTER
with colophon is a registered trademark of Penguin
Random House LLC.

ISBN 978-0-593-23294-1

Printed in China

Conceived and compiled by Dian G. Smith and
Robie Rogge

Design by Lise Sukhu
Illustrations by Josh Brill and Lise Sukhu

10 9 8 7 6 5 4 3 2 1

First Edition